D1130407

MONROEVILLE PUBLIC LIBRARY
4000 GATEWAY CAMPUS BLVD
MONROEVILLE, PA 15146

SUPERSTARS
of
PRO
FOOTBALL

TROY POLAMALU

Jim Whiting

Mason Crest Publishers

MONROEVILLE PUBLIC

JAN 3 0 2009

LIBRARY

92 POL

Produced by OTTN Publishing in association with
21st Century Publishing and Communications, Inc.

Copyright © 2009 by Mason Crest Publishers. All rights reserved. No part of this publication may be reproduced or transmitted in any form or by any means, electronic or mechanical, including photocopying, recording, taping, or any information storage and retrieval system, without permission from the publisher.

MASON CREST PUBLISHERS INC.
370 Reed Road
Broomall, Pennsylvania 19008
(866) MCP-BOOK (toll free)
www.masoncrest.com

Printed in the United States of America.

First Printing

9 8 7 6 5 4 3 2 1

Library of Congress Cataloging-in-Publication Data

Whiting, Jim, 1943-
   Troy Polamalu / Jim Whiting.
      p. cm. — (Superstars of pro football)
   Includes bibliographical references.
ISBN-13: 978-1-4222-0554-9 (hardcover) — ISBN-10: 1-4222-0554-1 (hardcover)
ISBN-13: 978-1-4222-0833-5 (pbk.) — ISBN-10: 1-4222-0833-8 (pbk.)
   1. Polamalu, Troy, 1981–   —Juvenile literature. 2. Football players—United States—Biography—Juvenile literature. I. Title.
GV939.P65W55 2008
796.332092—dc22
[B]   2008028190

Publisher's note:
All quotations in this book come from original sources, and contain the spelling and grammatical inconsistencies of the original text.

◀◀ CROSS-CURRENTS ▶▶

In the ebb and flow of the currents of life we are each influenced by many people, places, and events that we directly experience or have learned about. Throughout the chapters of this book you will come across **CROSS-CURRENTS** reference bubbles. These bubbles direct you to a **CROSS-CURRENTS** section in the back of the book that contains fascinating and informative sidebars and related pictures. Go on. ▶▶

◀◀CONTENTS▶▶

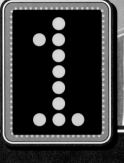

SUPER BOWL CHAMPION

In the days leading up to Super Bowl XL on February 5, 2006, Etric Pruitt of the Seattle Seahawks wore a red jersey during his team's practices. Normally a red jersey serves as a clear warning, saying, "Stop! Don't hit this player!" Quarterbacks usually wear red jerseys during practice, so they don't get roughed up. Pruitt, however, was a **defensive back**.

Pruitt was wearing the jersey because he was assigned to imitate Pittsburgh Steelers strong **safety** Troy Polamalu. The red jersey helped the quarterback prepare for Troy's incredible moves.

It is very unusual for a safety to receive this kind of "star treatment" during an opposing team's practice, but Troy is not a typical

Pittsburgh Steelers safety Troy Polamalu speaks to reporters the week before Super Bowl XL. Troy's team would face off against the Seattle Seahawks at Detroit's Ford Field for the NFL title.

safety. According to John Madden, a former National Football League (NFL) coach and a sports **analyst**:

❝ [Troy] does things no one else has done in the history of pro football. ❞

CROSS-CURRENTS

For a brief look at how the safety position fits into football defenses, see page 46. ▶▶

Madden's words were high praise for a player who had entered the NFL just three years earlier. Since then, Troy had emerged as one of the league's most feared safeties. He had been named to the All-Pro team and the Pro Bowl—the league's all-star game—twice. Troy was also one of the main reasons why the Steelers advanced to the Super Bowl.

Troy Polamalu goes airborne to help teammate Ike Taylor bring down Seattle Seahawks wide receiver Darrell Jackson during Super Bowl XL, February 5, 2006. The Steelers' defense held Seattle to just one touchdown and a field goal, and Pittsburgh won, 21–10.

Distinctive Look and Play

Troy's long black hair has helped make him one of the league's most recognizable players. His hair flows out from under his helmet and covers much of the back of his jersey. The last time he cut it was in 2000. Troy keeps his hair long to honor his Samoan heritage. Historically, Samoan men have had long hair.

Troy's long hair may be distinctive, but what really sets him apart from the NFL's other top safeties—and what attracted Madden's praise—is the way he plays his position. As a strong safety, Troy lines up opposite the other team's tight end, the "strong" side of the offensive line. That doesn't mean, however, that Troy stays there.

Troy is nicknamed the "Tasmanian Devil" because he's in constant motion before the ball is snapped and because of his ferocious tackling. As sportswriter Tom Silverstein pointed out in the *Milwaukee Journal Sentinel*:

❝There isn't a safety in the NFL who pursues the ball with the desire Polamalu does, and few are as fundamentally sound. The Steelers utilize Polamalu in so many facets of their blitz scheme that it's next to impossible to know exactly from what direction he's coming.❞

Nunyo Demasio of *Sports Illustrated* adds:

❝[Troy has] more disguises than someone on the FBI's most wanted list. My favorite bit of chicanery is when Polamalu turns his back to the offense as if returning to the secondary following a fake blitz. He then whirls around and joins the pass rush.❞

A Man on the Move

Standing on the sideline, former Steelers offensive guard Alan Faneca has an ideal vantage point from which he can appreciate Troy's talents:

❝Sometimes he'll run from deep safety 20 yards down, pop out to the right side, 25, 30 yards out there, then come flying back across the field and make a pick. I mean, the guy ran 80 yards—and the play hasn't even started yet.❞

Because Troy is always on the move, opposing teams have to account for him on every play.

But even accounting for Troy might not be enough. Troy played a key role in a playoff game against the Indianapolis Colts and their future Hall of Fame quarterback Peyton Manning. This game led up to the Super Bowl. The Associated Press (AP) noted:

CROSS-CURRENTS

The Super Bowl is pro football's biggest stage. For some information on the game's history, see
page 47. ▶▶

> **"**The Steelers used Polamalu in so many ways— bringing him off the edge as a rush linebacker, slipping him into pass protection, or blitzing him up the middle— that Manning could be seen looking for him on nearly every play. The blitzes so disrupted Manning that he complained afterward about his lack of protection.**"**

Red Means "Beware"

The Seahawks wanted to prevent the same thing from happening to them. That was why they assigned Pruitt to watch hours of Pittsburgh game film. Pruitt studied Troy, so he could imitate the way Troy was likely to move. Pruitt's red jersey made it easier for

Troy Polamalu (seated, front) and some of his teammates wave to the throngs of people who turned out in downtown Pittsburgh for the Steelers' Super Bowl XL victory parade, February 7, 2006.

Seahawks quarterback Matt Hasselbeck to find Pruitt as the team practiced, so Hasselbeck could make split-second adjustments.

Pruitt's efforts proved to be partially successful. Sportswriter Dan Pompei notes that during the Super Bowl:

> **❝The Seahawks' only touchdown came on a play in which they took advantage of [Troy]. Polamalu was responsible for Seahawks tight end Jerramy Stevens, and the Seahawks freed Stevens by having another receiver run between him and Polamalu. The result was a 16-yard touchdown pass.❞**

Apart from that one lapse, Troy was still, according to sportswriter Jim Corbett, "the most valuable defensive chess piece" in the Steelers' 21–10 victory.

Troy certainly justified that praise midway through the final quarter when Seattle was deep in Pittsburgh's territory. A touchdown would have given Seattle the lead. Hasselbeck threw toward the end zone, but Troy was blitzing, and his pressure forced Hasselbeck to hurry his pass. Steelers cornerback Ike Taylor intercepted the pass.

The Steelers took advantage of this turnover and eventually scored, putting the game out of reach for the Seahawks. Soon afterward, Troy and his teammates received the prize every pro football player wants: the jewel-encrusted Super Bowl championship ring.

The ring marked the **culmination** of a process that began when Troy was just eight years old. Troy had to make a choice few children his age face. His decision set him on the path that led to the Super Bowl.

TEN YEARS IN TENMILE

Troy Polamalu Aumua was born on April 19, 1981, in Garden Grove, a town in Orange County, California, just outside of Los Angeles. He was the youngest of five children. Troy's parents split up when he was an infant, and the family's situation appeared to have a negative effect on his siblings. They were often in trouble, and Troy was well on the way to following their lead.

By the age of eight, Troy had started smoking. He often stole his lunch from a nearby grocery store, and he broke into houses. One time, Troy took a woman's dog. When she posted a reward for its return, Troy brought the animal back and pocketed the reward money.

At about this time, Troy's mother decided to visit her brother, Salu Polamalu, in the tiny town of Tenmile, Oregon. Tenmile had a population of less than 200 and was named for its 10-mile distance from Winston, a slightly larger town with just a few thousand residents. The area's high school, where Troy would eventually become a three-sport star, had barely 400 students. Troy was struck by how different this place appeared to be:

> **I saw cows in the pasture, horses, the sun. And man, it must've just rained, 'cause everything was green.**

The Lure of the Outdoors

While in Tenmile, Troy went waterskiing on a nearby lake with his cousins. He headed deep into the forest on camping trips and fished off a dock. Troy fell in love with the place, and he begged his mother to let him stay with Salu. Even at a young age, Troy knew he didn't

Troy Polamalu came into his own as an athlete in high school. He was a standout in three sports: baseball, basketball, and football, but football was his favorite.

During a family visit to relatives in the small community of Tenmile, Oregon, Troy Polamalu fell in love with the outdoors. He convinced his mother to let him remain with his aunt and uncle in Tenmile when the rest of the family returned to California.

want to go back to a troubled community. Staying, however, meant being separated from his mother and siblings. It was a tough choice.

Salu and his wife, Kelley, made a financial sacrifice and agreed to take in Troy. He, in essence, became their fourth son. Salu was aware of how momentous Troy's decision was:

> **❝[Troy's] so intelligent. He made a decision not to go back to a place where he saw violence and gangs as a way of life. He sacrificed being around his mom, his brother and three sisters. What young man is willing to say he would do that, I don't know. It's fascinating that someone that young would make a decision like that.❞**

Troy appreciated what his uncle and his mother had done for him. He noted:

> **"**[Salu] is a disciplinarian and kept me straight. . . . It was a great move for me. My mom wanted the best for me. I think [it was] a very selfless decision my mother made. A lot of my siblings and cousins had fallen into adversity.**"**

Samoan Family Values

In Samoan culture, a move like Troy's is not uncommon. Samoans have a particularly strong sense of family unity. Salu was the chief of his family, and in a long-standing tradition, the chief is responsible for keeping the family united, even members of the extended family.

Although the Polamalus were the only Samoan family in the area, Salu made sure Troy learned the Samoan values of family unity, personal **integrity**, and strict discipline. Troy had to do well in school and help with chores at home.

Above all, Troy had to be humble. He once spiked the football during a youth league game, and Salu immediately yanked him off the field. Troy got the message. Later, he said:

> **"**I knew that I had it tough compared to children around me. But I felt like I needed it.**"**

Salu's "tough love" helped Troy. Lee Jenkins of the *New York Times* noted:

> **"**Polamalu became a straight-A student, spent free time playing with mentally disabled students in the special-education program, and flourished in the wood-shop. He built coffee tables and treasure chests, carved Polynesian symbols into the wood and won ribbons in local contests for his pieces. Then he would give them away to family members and friends as gifts.**"**

A New Name

Troy's gratitude to his uncle eventually took a more concrete form. A few years after he began living in Tenmile, he changed his name to Troy Polamalu.

By then, Troy was also going through another change. He was becoming more committed to the Christian faith, another part of Samoan culture. Troy found that this faith reinforced his uncle's teachings about being humble. Troy's woodshop teacher, Jim Anderson, noted:

"[Troy] was probably better than anybody else at almost every subject, but he never acted that way. He never thought of himself as being different from anyone."

Playing at a Different Level

To others, however, Troy was different when it came to sports. Rick Taylor, Troy's football coach at Douglas High School, pointed out that Troy seemed to have something extra on the field. Taylor said many people who saw Troy play believed he'd make it into the NFL.

Josh Bidwell, a Douglas graduate who also became a pro football player, was one of those early believers. He often played basketball with Troy. Troy was usually the youngest player on the court, but that didn't matter, Bidwell reported:

CROSS-CURRENTS

The independent nation of Samoa has a population of less than a quarter million. With about 67,000 residents, American Samoa, a territory administered by the United States, is even smaller. But Samoans have loomed large in the NFL. See page 48 for details. ▶▶

"Troy killed us. He could shoot with his right hand or left hand and did whatever he wanted to do. . . . I said from day one that he would be the best athlete we'd ever see."

Despite his great athletic skills, Troy remained humble. Aaron Shoop, a boyhood friend and high school teammate, said Troy was down-to-earth and never acted like he was a star.

At Douglas High School, Troy was All-League in basketball twice, and he did even better in baseball. As a senior, he garnered All-State honors, playing center field and batting a whopping .550.

It was in football, however, that Troy shone the brightest. He made the varsity team as a freshman, and he rushed for more than 1,000 yards as both a sophomore and a junior. He seemed ready to have an even more phenomenal year as a senior. In his first four games, he rushed for nearly 700 yards. Several major injuries, however, stopped him from playing.

Still, Troy made many memorable plays at Douglas. During one play, he started left, found his way blocked, and cut back to his right to score a touchdown. This play was called back because of a penalty, but on the very next play, Troy took the ball, headed right, cut back to the left, and scored again!

Troy was just as impressive on defense. Coach Taylor noted:

> **You'd put him back defensively, and it was like having two free safeties. . . . he could cover the whole field. . . . I remember Troy got called once for hitting too hard. It wasn't an illegal hit or anything else, he just hit too hard. Troy made a good, clean hit, but it was just so hard that it looked like there had to be something wrong.**

By this time, Troy had developed his characteristic approach to the game. As Justin Myers, another friend, recalled:

> **To hear him talk and then to see him play, he was two different people. People may think he plays crazy and reckless now, but he played the same way back in high school. He was a soft-spoken, mild-mannered guy in the lockerroom, but then a ferocious, intense guy on the field.**

Although Troy only played four games his senior year, Super Prep, a college **recruiting** service, noticed his talent. The service named him to its All-Northwest Team. The *Tacoma News Tribune* put him on its Western 100 team.

When Troy graduated in 1999, he was ready to take his ferocity and intensity to the next level. Soon the rest of the nation would find out what the people in southwest Oregon already knew.

TROY THE USC TROJAN

For a while, it wasn't entirely clear that Troy would have a future in college football. Tenmile, Oregon, was well off the beaten track for college **scouts**. High schools in his area didn't appear to have very competitive football teams, and Troy didn't have highlight film of himself in action to show the scouts.

One factor, however, was in Troy's favor. Some of Troy's relatives had had impressive football careers. Troy's uncle, Kennedy Pola, played at the University of Southern California (USC) and later became an assistant coach at the University of Colorado. After Troy's junior year, Pola urged Colorado's head coach, Rick Neuheisel, to invite his nephew to Colorado's summer camp.

Pola told Neuheisel that the coach would want to offer Troy a football scholarship after seeing him play. Troy didn't disappoint his uncle. Pola notes:

> **❝So he goes out there, runs the fastest 40, verticals the highest, plays WR [wide receiver], S [safety], RB [running back]. Neuheisel, before the day's over, pulls him into his office and offers him a scholarship.❞**

Troy probably would have taken the offer, but Neuheisel left Colorado the following January for the University of Washington, and he apparently lost interest in Troy. Pola also left Colorado for a job at San Diego State. Pola, however, urged Paul Hackett, the head coach at USC, to take a look at Troy.

The University of Southern California football team gets pumped up before the start of a game. Troy Polamalu attended USC on a football scholarship, enrolling in the fall of 1999.

Kennedy Pola, Troy Polamalu's uncle. It was Pola, a former player at USC, who convinced Trojans head coach Paul Hackett to recruit Troy. Pola also served as an assistant coach at USC during Troy's sophomore, junior, and senior years.

The Thundering Herd

USC has one of the most historic college football programs in the country. The USC Trojans began playing football in 1888 and won four national titles during a 15-year span just before World War II. The team soon became known as "the Thundering Herd."

The Thundering Herd, however, was corralled for 20 years, until the arrival of coach John McKay in 1960. Under McKay, the school became a powerhouse again and won four national titles. When McKay left in 1976, his replacement, John Robinson, won another national title. During this time, the school produced four running backs who won the Heisman Trophy, earning USC another nickname: "Tailback University."

The school also developed some of the nation's best safeties. Trojans Ronnie Lott, Dennis Smith, Mark Carrier, Dennis Thurman, and Tim McDonald were All-Americans at least once and had outstanding professional careers.

When Robinson left in 1982, the team began a long decline. In the 1990s, USC was the only team in college football's **Pac-10 Conference** that didn't win the conference championship at least once. Paul Hackett became coach in 1998, but under him, the Trojans didn't do much better.

Top players that the university might have attracted during better times were going to other colleges. That situation may have made Hackett more willing to take a look at Troy. Hackett offered Troy a scholarship—the last one available.

No Redshirting

Most freshmen in major college football programs are "redshirted." Redshirted players practice with the team, but they don't play in any games. One of the main reasons that freshmen are redshirted is that the college game is so much faster than high school football. Most 18-year-olds can't compete effectively at that level. While they are redshirted, freshmen have the benefit of a full year of practice before starting to play. They also can play for the next four seasons—adding a year to their college career.

With his relatively unknown background, Troy was very likely to be redshirted his freshman year, but he had other ideas. Troy wanted to work hard to make a name for himself.

Troy knew he would have to learn new techniques, including techniques that players from more prestigious high school programs already knew. He decided to focus on one skill in particular. Troy noted:

> **"The thing that's really hard to teach somebody is how to hit. So when I came into freshman camp, all I wanted to do was hit. I really didn't have any idea of what I was doing, but I knew I was going to hit someone as hard as I could. . . . [Hitting], that's where my success started."**

Troy may well have been the team's least-recruited player, but in his mind, that didn't matter on the field:

" I had to establish that everyone on the practice field was equal. They threw a bad pass and [receiver] R. Jay Soward—he was the big star at the time—was kind of trotting through his route, and I went over and blindsided him. He got up cussing me, but later he told me I was okay. I think that got me noticed a little bit. **"**

Making an Immediate Impact

That little bit of notice was all Troy needed. Soon, it was apparent he wouldn't be redshirted. Troy saw action as a reserve safety and linebacker and also on **special teams**. He played in eight games. He missed four games because of a concussion he suffered in practice.

Football wasn't Troy's only focus. He also became active in Polynesian clubs at USC, and he learned how to speak Samoan and to do traditional Samoan dances. When the season ended, Troy traveled to American Samoa to visit his mother, who had remarried and moved there a few years earlier.

The following year, Troy became a starter at strong safety. He intercepted a pass in the season opener against Penn State and dashed 43 yards for a touchdown. He ended the season as the Trojans' second-leading tackler with 83 tackles, including 14 against both Notre Dame and Arizona State.

Hitting Bottom

Troy may have been doing well, but his team was not. The Trojans went just 2–6 in conference play and finished last for the first time in their history. A coaching change seemed necessary. Hackett was let go, but the university had a difficult time finding his replacement.

Almost in desperation, the school turned to Pete Carroll. Many fans were upset. Carroll hadn't coached at the college level in nearly 20 years.

In 2001, Carroll's first year and Troy's junior year, the Trojans didn't get off to a good start. USC won just two of its first seven games. Troy, however, played outstanding football. By this time, he had impressed his teammates so much

CROSS-CURRENTS

After Troy's sophomore season, USC tapped Pete Carroll to be its new head football coach. For a profile of the man who brought two national championships to USC, see page 49. ▶▶

Troy Polamalu runs back an interception for a touchdown in USC's 2000 season opener against Penn State. The Trojans won the game, played at Giants Stadium in East Rutherford, New Jersey, by a score of 29–5.

that they chose him as one of the team's captains, an honor that is almost always reserved for seniors. Carroll, a defensive specialist, proved to be a good **mentor**.

The Trojans caught fire during the season's second half. They had a four-game winning streak and went on to play Utah in the Las Vegas Bowl. Although Troy made a career-high 20 tackles in the game, the Trojans lost, 10–6.

Troy finished the season with a team-best 118 tackles; he was the Trojans' leading tackler in 8 of their 12 games. He also blocked three punts and intercepted three passes, returning two for touchdowns. Troy was named to numerous All-American teams.

Senior Year

Going into the 2002 season, Troy's senior year, USC was ranked number 19 in the nation in the ESPN/USA Today preseason poll. The Associated Press preseason poll ranked the Trojans number 18 nationally. Pac-10 sportswriters didn't think the team was that good: they predicted that USC would finish fourth in the conference.

USC players and coaches, however, had a more positive outlook. Defensive tackle Shaun Cody predicted that the team would not lose a game in conference play. Carroll was just as optimistic:

> **❝The guys that light me up are the seniors. [Quarterback] Carson Palmer is so pumped up about this season. So are guys like Troy Polamalu and [linebacker] Mike Pollard. These are guys you look toward for senior leadership to give you a chance to have a good football team and a big year.❞**

Nearly halfway through the 2002 season, however, that optimism appeared unjustified. After a 30–27 loss at Washington State University (WSU), the Trojans were just 3–2. In Pac-10 Conference play, they were 1–1.

There was, however, a reason why the Trojans had struggled against WSU, a team they usually beat. Troy suffered an ankle sprain early in the game, and he couldn't play. The injury also kept him out of the next game as the Trojans eked out a two-point win over California.

2002 USC FOOTBALL

THE RETURN OF TROY

TROY POLAMALU

2001 ALL-AMERICAN SAFETY
2002 THORPE AWARD CANDIDATE
WEARING NEW USC ROAD JERSEY

USC's 2002 football preview magazine featured senior Troy Polamalu on its cover. During his junior year, the hard-hitting safety had recorded 118 tackles and been picked as an All-American.

Troy returned to action against the University of Washington the following week. In that game he made an interception, and the Trojans won, 41–21. With Troy back in the lineup, USC overwhelmed its final five opponents and ended the season on a high note. In Pac-10 play, the Trojans finished 7–1, which tied them with WSU for the conference title.

In addition, the Trojans had, for the first time in 21 years, beaten their traditional rivals Notre Dame and UCLA in the same season. Some people believed USC was the best team in the country by the end of the 2002 season. However, because of the early-season losses, the Trojans finished the season ranked number five in the nation.

A University of Colorado running back finds out just how hard Troy Polamalu can hit, September 14, 2002. USC dominated the game, blowing the Buffaloes away by a score of 40–3.

Troy finished the year second on the team in tackles, with 68. But Carroll was quick to point out that numbers by themselves barely hinted at his value to the team:

"He's an incredible football player who has tremendous instincts. He knows when to take his shots. We use him a number of ways to feature his talents. There is nothing he can't do real well. You can't put a value on what he means to this team."

A Bowl Game

On January 2, 2003, the Trojans played the third-ranked University of Iowa Hawkeyes in the Orange Bowl. Unfortunately, Troy pulled a muscle in practice a few days before the game and couldn't play. Even without Troy, however, USC crushed the Hawkeyes, 38–17.

It was clear that Trojan football was back on track. Carson Palmer, Troy's roommate, not only was the Orange Bowl's Most Valuable Player, but he also became the first Trojan since 1981 to win the Heisman Trophy.

Once again, Troy was named to many All-American teams. He was also one of three finalists for the Jim Thorpe Award, which is given to the nation's best defensive back.

Troy was ready to take his skills to the next level. This time, however, he was no longer an obscure player from a small Oregon town. Now he was a well-known face in one of the top football programs in the country.

Only two questions remained: which NFL team would **draft** Troy, and when would he be picked?

CROSS-CURRENTS

The Heisman Trophy is awarded each year to the best college football player in the nation. Seven USC players have won the Heisman. To find out who they are, *see page 50.* ▶▶

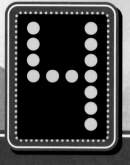

RISING TO THE TOP

In the 2003 NFL draft, the Pittsburgh Steelers were prepared to do something they had never done before: pick a safety in the first round. The team had won its division in 2001 and 2002. In both years, the Steelers had boasted the NFL's best defense against the run.

When opponents passed the ball, however, it was a different story. The Steelers' pass defense had slipped from number 4 in 2001 to number 20 in 2002. As the Steelers prepared for the 2003 draft, strengthening the secondary was their main concern. They needed a good safety.

Almost every draft board listed Troy as the top college safety, and Troy quickly rose to the top of the Steelers' wish list. In pre-draft workouts, he clocked 4.35 in the 40-yard dash,

At USC, Troy Polamalu had shown himself to be equally adept at stopping the run and covering receivers. It was primarily Troy's coverage skills that attracted the Pittsburgh Steelers, who selected him in the first round of the 2003 NFL draft.

a time that only a few players surpassed. With a vertical leap of 43 inches, his ability to jump up and slap the ball away from receivers was unquestionable.

A Tough Trade

In the NFL's draft system, teams choose in the reverse order of their previous year's finish. The Steelers' success in 2002 meant that 26 teams would pick before them. They were afraid Troy would be gone before it was their turn to pick.

The team, therefore, did something else for the first time: it traded up to get the player it wanted. Pittsburgh traded its number 27 pick in the first round, plus its third- and sixth-round selections, for the Kansas City Chiefs' 16th overall pick.

It was a steep price to pay, and there was no guarantee that Troy would fulfill the team's expectations. The history of the NFL draft is littered with first-round picks who failed to pan out. The Steelers, however, were willing to take the risk.

The Steelers' announcement of Troy Polamalu as their selection set off an uproar at the home of Troy's uncle. Kennedy Pola had invited many of Troy's relatives and friends to a draft-day party. After hearing the pick, everyone rushed into the backyard and joined in the Paualuga, a Samoan celebration dance.

Pittsburgh's Heinz Field was the site of Troy Polamalu's NFL debut. In the game—which was played on September 7, 2003—the hometown Steelers beat the Baltimore Ravens by a score of 34–15. But Pittsburgh struggled during the 2003 season, and so did Troy.

Pola's high expectations for Troy matched the Steelers'. Pola explained:

> **"[Troy] plays for his faith, and he plays for his culture— the Samoan people. He's a man of God. He's family oriented, but, on the field, he lays it all out. He gives everything he has."**

In one sense, Pittsburgh was similar to Tenmile. Hardly any Samoans lived there. This time, however, there was no close family to welcome and help sustain Troy. He noted:

> **"It's sort of how you would feel if you were dropped off in the middle of the Congo.... It was a pretty big shock."**

Rough Rookie Year

Some people expected Troy to step into the Steelers' starting lineup right away, but Troy didn't. As Troy recalled, he struggled to learn the team's complex defensive game plans:

> **"My rookie year was very tough because they pretty much had me do everything.... I gave up a lot of plays because I didn't know what I was doing. For me, I have to learn something with repetition because I try to make everything instinctual for myself. Some things took a lot more time for me to learn."**

Troy wasn't the only Steeler to struggle. In 2003, Pittsburgh didn't come close to repeating its successes from the two previous years. The team won just 6 games and lost 10.

One high point for Troy was that he led the special teams in tackles. At the end of the season, he received the Joe Greene Great Performance Award, given annually to Pittsburgh's top rookie. With his typical humility, Troy downplayed its significance, saying he was the only rookie to see substantial playing time.

Also typically, Troy spent the off-season watching endless hours of game film to help him learn his position. He watched moves made by John Lynch of Denver, Ed Reed of Baltimore, and

Sean Taylor of Washington, players he regarded as the league's best safeties.

New Coach, New Season

As the team prepared for the 2004 season, it quickly became obvious that Troy's long hours of film study had paid off. Troy also benefited from a coaching change. After the disappointing 2003 season, the Steelers hired Dick LeBeau as defensive coordinator. LeBeau quickly realized that Troy could be a great weapon on defense:

> **"He gives you unlimited flexibility. He can play the deep perimeter. He can play as a linebacker support player. He can blitz. For a defensive coordinator, he's ideal. You can put him anyplace."**

Lebeau made Troy a starter. It didn't take long for Chris Hope, the Steelers' other starting safety and Troy's best friend on the team, to give him the nickname "Tasmanian Devil":

> **"It goes with the way his hair goes all over the place and the way he runs. He's always into something. If you look at our film, he's always diving, scratching, clawing under a pile. He's always full speed, going 125 miles per hour."**

LeBeau's confidence in Troy paid off. He was named to the Associated Press All-Pro second team, and he played in his first Pro Bowl.

Troy's play on the field was one major reason why the Steelers made a dramatic turnaround after their dismal 2003 season. The team went 15-1 in the regular season and reached the AFC championship game before losing to the New England Patriots, the eventual Super Bowl champions.

The play of rookie Ben Roethlisberger was another reason for Pittsburgh's success. In the 2004 draft, the Steelers had used their first-round pick (the 11th pick overall) to take Roethlisberger, a quarterback. After becoming the starter in the third game of the season, he turned in one of the greatest rookie years in NFL history.

Troy Polamalu is hauled down by Cleveland Browns wide receiver Antonio Bryant, November 14, 2004. Troy had saved a touchdown by picking off a Jeff Garcia pass intended for Bryant at the Pittsburgh two-yard line.

Getting Married

Troy was disappointed his team hadn't made it to the Super Bowl, but he didn't have much time to brood. In late January 2005, Troy married Theodora Holmes, the sister of USC teammate Alex Holmes.

Alex said he remembered when Troy first asked for his permission to date Theodora. "I couldn't have been happier," Alex noted. "He's such an exceptional person."

One of the things Troy liked about Theodora was that she was not a football fan. Troy noted:

> **"It's nice to be able to come home and not have my wife tell me that I missed my read in Cover-6, you know what I mean?"**

The foundation for their marriage, however, goes much deeper. Theodora belongs to the Greek Orthodox Church. While Troy had been deeply religious for many years, he hadn't yet found a permanent church. He soon joined his new wife as a Greek Orthodox.

High Hopes

With their rookie quarterback now seasoned by a year of experience, Pittsburgh fans looked forward to a great 2005 season. The Steelers got off to a good start, winning seven of their first nine games.

A loss in overtime to the Baltimore Ravens, however, and two more defeats put the Steelers' playoff hopes on the line. The team rallied. Troy played a significant role in helping the team win its last four regular-season games. In these games, the defense held its opponents to just 33 points—slightly more than one touchdown per game.

Still, Pittsburgh was the sixth seed, the lowest rank for teams entering the playoffs. Every playoff game would be on the road. The Steelers, however, beat Cincinnati, 31–17, in the wild card round and then faced the top-seeded Indianapolis Colts.

With his team leading 21–10 late in the final quarter, Troy made an acrobatic dive to intercept a pass by Colts quarterback Peyton Manning. The Colts, however, challenged the ruling that the play was an interception. After the referee viewed the play again using the NFL's instant replay system, he agreed with the Colts.

Indianapolis went on to score a touchdown. But the Steelers hung on and beat the Colts, 21–18. NFL officials later said reversing Troy's interception was incorrect. Pittsburgh could have won handily.

Road to the Super Bowl

The Steelers then faced the Denver Broncos to compete for the AFC championship. The Broncos were undefeated at home that year, but it hardly seemed to matter. Pittsburgh had a 24–3 lead by halftime and coasted to a 34–17 win. The Steelers were set to play in Super Bowl XL.

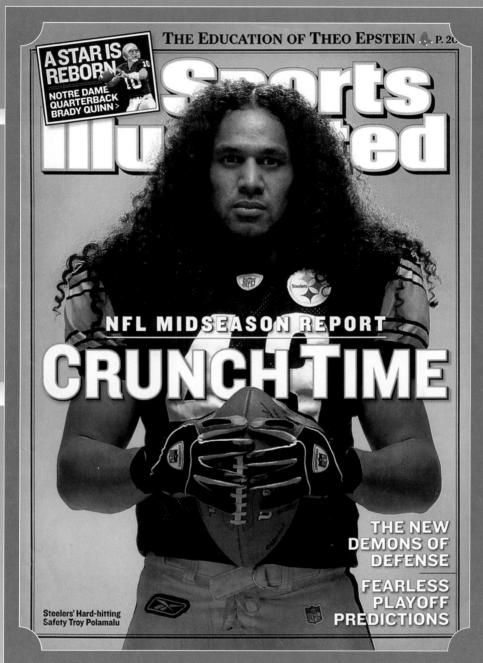

THE EDUCATION OF THEO EPSTEIN ♦ P. 20

A STAR IS REBORN
NOTRE DAME QUARTERBACK BRADY QUINN >

Sports Illustrated

NFL MIDSEASON REPORT

CRUNCH TIME

THE NEW DEMONS OF DEFENSE

FEARLESS PLAYOFF PREDICTIONS

Steelers' Hard-hitting Safety Troy Polamalu

The hard-hitting Troy Polamalu was an appropriate choice for the cover of *Sports Illustrated*'s 2005 midseason football report, which was titled "Crunch Time." Troy was doing more than just hitting, however. On November 6, for example, he returned a Green Bay Packers fumble 77 yards for a touchdown.

During the Denver game, once again, Troy had been in the middle of the action. Sportswriter Judy Battista noted in the *New York Times*:

CROSS-CURRENTS

With five Super Bowl victories, the Pittsburgh Steelers are one of the most successful franchises in NFL history. For a brief look at the team, turn to page 51. ▶▶

"Polamalu tackled Denver running back Tatum Bell a yard short of a first down, while Polamalu was being blocked and was falling down. Later, Polamalu nearly tackled running back Mike Anderson for a safety on a screen pass on third-and-10—even though Polamalu was responsible for covering a deep pass in the seam."

Troy Polamalu upends Denver Broncos running back Mike Anderson on the Denver one-yard line during the AFC championship game, January 22, 2006. The Steelers won, 34–17, thus earning a trip to Super Bowl XL.

The play on Bell was so astonishing that it was featured in many preview shows before the Super Bowl. To Troy, however, it wasn't astonishing at all:

"I was out of position actually on that play. I should have made the play sooner than that."

Almost at Home

The Steelers had proven themselves road warriors. The three playoff wins and two of the Steelers' final three regular-season games were played on the road. For the Super Bowl, however, the team enjoyed what was almost a homecoming. Although Super Bowl XL was played at Detroit, *USA Today* sportswriter Larry Weisman pointed out:

"No question [the Steelers] enjoyed the home-field advantage, and not just on Sunday. Everywhere they went, they saw their colors carried or worn by vociferous fans of the Black & Gold. Their numbers dwarfed those of the Seattle fans. It would not have been surprising to find out that Super Bowl XL was being contested by two teams called the Steelers, so numerous were their supporters."

The Steelers beat the Seattle Seahawks, 21–10, and came home to a celebratory parade. During the parade, Troy twice hopped off the truck that was carrying him and his teammates. He leapt into the sea of adoring fans who happily surfed him along.

Troy had produced a phenomenal 2005 season. He had 100 tackles during the regular season. He also recorded three sacks and two interceptions, and he forced a fumble. He was named a first-team All-Pro and was invited to his second Pro Bowl.

Pittsburgh and Troy seemed to be riding a wave.

A BRIGHT FUTURE

Several weeks into the 2006 season, Troy was involved in an unusual play. He intercepted a pass in the third quarter of a game against the Kansas City Chiefs. Troy raced down the sideline, but Chiefs running back Larry Johnson caught up with him and dragged him down by his hair.

Steelers fans booed, but Johnson didn't see anything wrong with what he had done. He defended himself in a post-game interview:

"I mean, the dude had hair. What do you want me to do? They said that hair is part of the uniform the last time I checked. When I grabbed him, that's the only thing I could get my hands on. It's not like I was trying to jerk him down."

Johnson was correct. NFL rules say that hair extending out from under the helmet is part of the uniform. Johnson was penalized, but the penalty was for unsportsmanlike conduct done *after* the play. When the play was over, Johnson appeared to pull Troy to his feet by his hair. Johnson protested that his fingers had become entwined in Troy's hair. Troy shrugged it off:

"He can tackle me by my hair or ankles. . . . I understand the nature of the game. A lot of things like that can happen."

With help from teammate Larry Foote, Troy Polamalu wraps up Kansas City Chiefs running back Larry Johnson, October 15, 2006. During the game—a 45–7 Pittsburgh victory—Johnson turned the tables. After Troy had intercepted a pass, Johnson tackled him by the hair.

Troy's awkward tumble to the turf appeared to symbolize the Steelers' entire 2006 season. The team beat Kansas City, but the win was just one of two in the Steelers' first eight games. The defending Super Bowl champions played better in the season's second half, but two losses to Baltimore ensured that Pittsburgh would miss the playoffs.

Troy, however, had another stellar season. Sportswriter Ron Cook of the *Pittsburgh Post-Gazette* noted a three-play sequence in a game against the Cleveland Browns that showed just how special Troy was:

Cleveland Browns quarterback Charlie Frye is forced to get rid of the ball to avoid being sacked by Troy Polamalu, November 19, 2006. The Steelers won the game, 24–20.

"[Troy] used his incredible closing speed on first down to run down Browns quarterback Charlie Frye for a sack in front of the Steelers' bench; displayed his toughness on second down by slicing through a mass of humanity to tackle running back Jason Wright after a 2-yard gain; and showed his marvelous football instincts on third down by pulling up on a blitz and leaping to bat down Frye's pass intended for [tight end Kellen] Winslow.**"**

The Browns were forced to punt after that play. The Steelers drove for a touchdown and a 24–20 victory.

Unfortunately, a knee injury caused Troy to miss three late-season games, but he was named to the Pro Bowl for the third year in a row and started for the second straight time.

Staying a Steeler

The Steelers took note of Troy's obvious value to the team. Before the 2007 season began, the Steelers made Troy the team's highest-paid player by giving him a $30 million **contract** extension through the 2011 season. They also, briefly, made him the league's highest-paid safety. (Troy lost that distinction several months later when Indianapolis signed Bob Sanders to a five-year, $37.5 million contract.)

Troy was especially happy because, unlike many other players, he prefers to play for a single team:

CROSS-CURRENTS

Troy Polamalu is one of the best safeties in the game today. For a look at some other standouts at that position, see page 52. ▶▶

"I didn't want to be a player who is jumping from team to team. I've always felt comfortable here. I think this organization, this tradition they have here, is very legendary, and I always wanted to be a part of this.**"**

In 2007, the Steelers came back from their disappointing 2006 season to finish the regular season with a 10–6 record. Unfortunately, the team lost to Jacksonville, 31–29, in the first round of the playoffs. Troy missed five games, including a three-game stretch just past mid-season, but he still received Associated Press second-team All-Pro honors. He also was named to his fourth Pro Bowl.

These honors capped an especially memorable year for Troy. He had become famous under the name Troy Polamalu, but his legal name was still his birth name, Troy Aumua. Early in 2007, he made his name change legal.

Caring for the Community

At about the same time, Troy and his wife announced the founding of the Harry Panos Fund, named after Theodora's grandfather. Panos had served in the military during World War II and had taken part in the U.S. invasions of the islands of Saipan and Okinawa.

The fund's objective is to assist young veterans after they return from the Iraq War. According to Theodora:

CROSS-CURRENTS

For information on the World War II battles for Saipan and Okinawa, turn to page 54. ▶▶

❝When Troy went to Washington, D.C., to receive accolades for the Super Bowl, he went to Walter Reed Hospital and met some of the wonderful young women veterans who had been severely injured by roadside bombs. Troy came home and told me, and after that discussion, we both agreed that veterans would be a good place to [focus a charitable fund].❞

Troy's involvement with charitable causes goes back to his early days with the team. In 2004, he participated in "Principal for a Day," sponsored by McDonald's restaurants. The elementary school that raised the most money for charity had Troy serve as "Principal for a Day."

The following year, Troy and Theodora were among the featured couples in Steelers Style 2005. This dinner and fashion show raised money for the Thomas E. Starzl Transplantation Institute at the University of Pittsburgh Medical Center and the Cancer Caring Center.

In 2006, Troy joined the NFL–United Way team. He filmed "The Wall," a commercial in which he helped teens climb a ladder next to a high stone barrier. The barrier symbolized the problems many teens face. Troy then said he'd like to help every teen who faces tough problems, but there are far too many of them for one person

Troy Polamalu celebrates Pittsburgh's Super Bowl victory with his wife, Theodora. The two are involved in a number of charitable efforts, including the Harry Panos Fund, which seeks to help soldiers returning from the war in Iraq. The fund is named after Theodora's grandfather, a World War II veteran.

to help. Troy's point was to encourage viewers to become involved in mentoring teens.

Not all of Troy's giving takes the form of organized charities. On one occasion, two women who knew nothing about football were seated next to Troy and Theodora at a restaurant. One of the women commented on Theodora's shoes, and before long the four were chatting happily. Troy's football exploits and fame never entered into the hour-long conversation. The Polamalus left the restaurant before the women. When the women went to pay their bill, the waiter said Troy had already paid it! This wasn't, however, the first time that he had paid for someone else's meal.

Troy also takes the time to visit critically ill people in the hospital or at their homes. He explains:

"You can truly save people's lives like that. . . . It's really beautiful in that way that you can affect people. In some ways, football is life here in Pittsburgh, it's their only hope."

A Church-going Couple

Troy hasn't neglected his spiritual side either. In the spring of 2007, Troy traveled to several Christian holy sites in Greece and Turkey with six other men from his church and two priests. He wanted to learn more about his faith.

Troy is also involved in his church's activities. One member notes:

CROSS-CURRENTS

Troy is a convert to the Eastern Orthodox faith. For a brief description of Eastern Orthodoxy, see page 54. ▶▶

"He participates in a lot of the services. He's even taken an active part in processions during Easter."

Troy attends church regularly with his wife. Because nearly all of his games are on Sunday, the couple goes to services at a Pittsburgh-area monastery on Tuesdays, Troy's day off from practice. The services begin at 8:30 and last for up to four hours. Troy doesn't find the amount of time excessive:

"What's really neat about the Orthodox church is that it's like walking back in time 2,000 years to the time of the **Apostles**, when they created these services. You walk into that, and it's really like . . . living it. . . . [W]e sit around there and meet with our spiritual mother."

Troy's spirituality extends to football. As he observes:

"I don't view football as a violent, barbaric sport. To me, it's a very spiritual sport, especially for the challenges a man faces within the game of football: the fear of failure, the fear of gaining too big of an ego, of making a mistake and everybody criticizing you."

This point of view even involves his nickname:

> **"**I know I have been identified as this crazy madman, as the 'Tasmanian Devil.' But I would rather be known as a 'Tasmanian Angel,' just a family man and a God-fearing man.**"**

Troy puts this belief on the field before every play. While many players are talking tough, trying to scare opponents, Troy breathes a silent prayer that no one will be injured.

An Unusual Player

With his quiet demeanor, ferocious play, and personal style, Troy appears destined to remain a fan favorite and one of the most well known faces of the Steelers. His contract extension is likely to keep

Troy Polamalu in a Nike ad. Since the Steelers' Super Bowl victory, Troy has been one of the NFL's more popular players. Through the 2007 regular season, his was the 10th-most purchased NFL jersey, according to *USA Today*.

In just a handful of seasons in the NFL, Troy Polamalu has established himself as one of the game's best safeties. Barring injury, the proud Samoan's career may one day lead to the Pro Football Hall of Fame.

him playing in Pittsburgh for most, if not all, of his professional career. If Troy stays healthy, that career could conclude with his election to the NFL's Hall of Fame.

Should that happen, Troy will almost certainly say that he knows the reason why. He explained in an interview:

> **With my life, there's no way that I could deny divine intervention. Coming where I've come from, the way that I've ended up at certain places where everything went just perfectly for me, whether it's here in Pittsburgh, with a perfect defensive scheme, or the way it was at USC, where Pete Carroll came in and kind of just gave me the whole defense and allowed me to become a first-round draft pick. It's just beautiful the way that it all worked out.**

Many NFL superstars thrive on a flashy lifestyle, flaunting their fame and wealth and boasting about their abilities. That has never been Troy's way. He is decidedly unassuming. Troy knows he doesn't fit the mold of a typical player. As he explains:

> **I do share different passions, you know: woodworking, flowers. I've started getting into orchids and trying to learn how to cultivate orchids. Wine. Trying to learn how to grow wine. Different things like that. Which, I guess, isn't your stereotypical football player, but different things interest me.**

For Troy Polamalu, breaking the mold has brought him a long way.

The Safety's Role

Most football defensive alignments, or formations, consist of four defensive linemen, three linebackers, two cornerbacks, and two safeties. The two cornerbacks and two safeties make up what is known as the secondary. Teams usually add more secondary players when they believe the opposing quarterback will be passing the ball.

In general, the cornerbacks are responsible for covering the other team's wide receivers. Cornerbacks need to be especially agile and fast. The safeties are the team's last line of defense. They try to make sure that no opposing players get past them. They usually are slightly taller and weigh more than the cornerbacks, and they often have reputations as ferocious tacklers. The strong safety normally lines up opposite the other team's tight end. Because the tight end provides an extra blocker on offense, his side of the offensive line is called the "strong side."

In many defensive plans, the strong safety covers the tight end. The strong safety also has to instantly recognize when the offensive team has called a running play, and he has to react immediately. He sometimes rushes the quarterback on a safety blitz.

The free safety commonly plays a little bit deeper than the strong safety. He is more likely to help the cornerbacks on deep pass plays. (Go back to page 5.) ◀◀

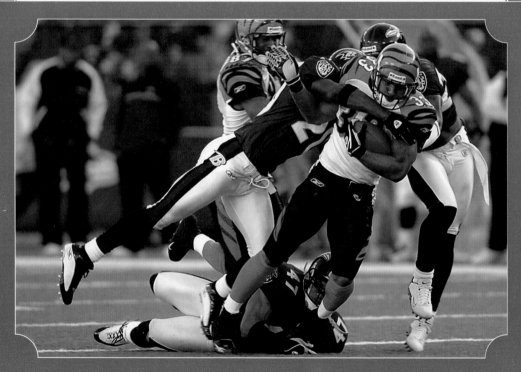

Baltimore Ravens free safety Ed Reed (#20, left) hits Cincinnati Bengals running back Kenny Watson during a 2004 game. Reed is one of the NFL's best at the safety position.

The Super Bowl

Although the first Super Bowl was played in 1967, its roots go back to 1960, when the American Football League (AFL) was formed to compete with the long-established National Football League (NFL). The AFL quickly became a strong rival to the older league.

By the mid-1960s, owners in both leagues were concerned that the competition between them was driving the players' salaries too high. The owners decided to merge the two leagues and form a single league. It would take several years to work out the details of the merger. One of the conditions, however, was that the winner of one league would play the winner of the other in a championship game.

The NFL's Most Famous Ball

At first, Pete Rozelle, the head of the NFL, wanted to call this game "The Big One." Then one day, Kansas City Chiefs owner Lamar Hunt came up with a different name. He was watching his children play with a Super Ball, and that toy gave him the idea of calling the game the "Super Bowl." He doubted this nickname would last very long, but he was wrong. Today, the Super Ball that the Hunt children played with is in the Professional Football Hall of Fame.

In the first Super Bowl in 1967, the Green Bay Packers easily defeated Lamar Hunt's Kansas City Chiefs, 35–10. The game's result was nearly the same the following year, with a 33–14 Packer win over the Oakland Raiders. These two wins seemed to confirm many fans' beliefs that the NFL had a higher quality of play.

The Namath Guarantee

In 1969, nearly everyone expected the third game to follow the same pattern. The NFL's Baltimore Colts were 18-point favorites over the AFL's New York Jets. Jets quarterback Joe Namath, however, guaranteed that his team would win. He backed up his words on the field, and his team emerged with a 16–7 win, one of the greatest upsets in American sports history. When the AFL champion Chiefs defeated the NFL champion Minnesota Vikings 23–7 the following year, doubts about the competitive differences between the leagues disappeared.

By the start of the 1970 season, the merger was complete. The new league was known as the National Football League. Its then-26 teams were divided into two conferences: the American Football Conference (AFC), which consisted of 10 AFL teams plus 3 former NFL teams, and the National Football Conference (NFC), which consisted of the 13 remaining NFL teams. From then on, the Super Bowl would match the two conference winners.

Today, the Super Bowl is the single most-watched television event in the United States. Super Bowl Sunday has almost become a national holiday.

(Go back to page 7.) ◀◀

Samoans and Football

The Samoan Islands are located in the Pacific Ocean between New Zealand and Hawaii. The much larger western group of islands makes up the independent nation of Samoa. The United States governs several small eastern islands, known as American Samoa. Some residents of American Samoa have moved to Hawaii or to the western coast of the United States.

Jack Thompson, nicknamed "the Throwin' Samoan," quarterbacked Washington State University in the late 1970s. By the time his college career was over, Thompson held the NCAA's all-time record for passing yardage. He did not, however, achieve stardom in the NFL.

Many Samoans in the United States have developed a love of football. Tui Alailefaleula, a Samoan who played football at the University of Washington, notes that football is "the sport we were born to play." He says through football, many Samoans can reach their goals and help their families.

The first Samoan to play football professionally was Al Lolotai of the Washington Redskins. He played in 1945. In the late 1970s, more Samoans began playing at the college level, particularly in the western states. They then entered the NFL.

Jack Thompson of Washington State was known as "the Throwin' Samoan." He set National Collegiate Athletic Association (NCAA) records for passing yardage. Manu Tuiasosopo starred at the University of California, Los Angeles (UCLA), while Mosi Tatupu was an outstanding blocking fullback at the University of Southern California (USC). All three players played in the NFL and have sons who followed them into the league.

As of 2008, more than 200 Samoans were playing Division 1 college football, and nearly 30 were on NFL rosters. Junior Seau, one of the greatest linebackers in NFL history, says that for Samoans, football success begins in childhood:

❝I honestly think it is tied to the work ethic within the home. Those intangibles of not taking anything for granted. For me, what my mom and dad instilled within me has helped me overcome obstacles and focus on the sport itself.❞

Marques Tuiasosopo, Manu's son and a professional quarterback, is grateful to his father and other early Samoan players. He says the first group of Samoans to make the league were role models for the next generation. He and his fellow Samoan players are a "by-product of the original dream of those early Samoans," Tuiasosopo notes.

❝Samoan kids can say, 'I can have a dream.' Whether they live in the cities or the suburbs, in American Samoa or [on] the mainland, they can see that there are Samoans accomplishing their dreams and living them out. To be able to see someone from the same ethnic background do well, it's kind of exciting.❞

(Go back to page 14.)

Pete Carroll

Born in 1951, Pete Carroll played football at the University of the Pacific and became a graduate coaching assistant there. He then began his first of several college assistant coaching jobs.

Carroll started coaching professional football in 1984. He served as an assistant coach with the NFL's Buffalo Bills, Minnesota Vikings, and New York Jets. In 1994, Carroll became the Jets' head coach, but he was fired after a single season. Three years later he became head coach of the New England Patriots. Carroll served as head coach for three years before again being fired.

In 2000, when USC was seeking a new head coach, the university offered the job to three coaches before settling on Carroll. Many prominent USC alumni opposed Carroll's hiring. When the Trojans started the 2001 season with a 2–5 record, the alumni's objections seemed well founded.

However, from that point through the end of the 2007 season, the Trojans compiled a phenomenal 74–9 record. They won one national championship and shared another. Between 2002 and 2007, the Trojans either won the Pac-10 Conference title outright or were conference co-champions.

Carroll has a reputation as a player-friendly coach. He tries to make practices enjoyable, and he sometimes plays practical jokes. Carroll also is active in charity work. He makes regular visits to neighborhoods affected by gangs, hoping to curb the cycle of gang violence.

(Go back to page 20.)

USC Heisman Trophy Winners

Every year sportswriters vote for nation's best college football player, who is honored with the Heisman Trophy. As of the 2007 season, USC has produced seven Heisman Trophy winners. The university is tied with Notre Dame and Ohio State for producing the most Heisman winners.

Mike Garrett (1965)

Mike Garrett started USC's "Tailback University" reputation. He became the first of four Trojan trophy winners in 16 years. Garrett led the nation in rushing, with 1,440 yards. He caught 36 passes, returned punts and kickoffs, and even threw two touchdown passes. Garrett eventually returned to USC as athletic director, and he hired Pete Carroll as coach.

O. J. Simpson (1968)

O. J. Simpson led the nation in rushing during each of his two years at USC. Simpson was the overwhelming choice for the Heisman Trophy during his senior year. His 2,853 points in the Heisman balloting, and his 1,750-point margin over the runner-up, were both records. In the NFL, Simpson became the first player to rush for more than 2,000 yards in a single season.

Charles White (1979)

By the time Charles White graduated, he held more than 20 NCAA, Pac-10 Conference, and USC records. He remains USC's all-time leading rusher. White's eight-year NFL career was a disappointment, however.

Marcus Allen (1981)

Marcus Allen was the first college running back to break the 2,000-yard barrier. He rushed for an astounding 2,342 yards. He was equally distinguished as a professional. Allen became the first NFL running back to amass 10,000 yards on the ground and 5,000 yards in pass receptions.

Carson Palmer (2002)

Carson Palmer earned the Heisman Trophy with a spectacular senior season. He set school records for pass completions (309), passing yards (3,942), and touchdown passes (33).

Matt Leinart (2004)

As a junior, Matt Leinart led the Trojans to an undefeated regular season. For the first time in history, two Heisman Trophy winners played against each other when Leinart and the Trojans took on Oklahoma and 2003 winner Barry White in the Orange Bowl. Leinart outplayed White, and USC took home the national championship.

Reggie Bush (2005)

Reggie Bush's electrifying play was simply off the charts. He was a threat to score every time he touched the football, whether he was rushing, catching passes, or returning punts and kickoffs.

(Go back to page 25.)

The Pittsburgh Steelers

In 1933, Art Rooney of Pittsburgh had a great day at the racetrack. He won $2,500 betting on horses. Rooney used his winnings to establish a team in the National Football League. The team was named the Pirates after Pittsburgh's long-established baseball team.

It took Rooney's team nearly 10 years to produce a winning record. By then, the team had become the Steelers, a name reflecting Pittsburgh's central place in the nation's steel industry. The Steelers finally made the playoffs in 1947, but they lost in the first round.

Getting Better

For the next 20 years the Steelers were mediocre. They hit rock bottom in 1968 and 1969, winning a total of just three games. The seeds of future greatness, however, were being sown.

Chuck Noll became coach before the 1969 season, and he chose defensive tackle "Mean" Joe Greene in the draft that year. The following year he took quarterback Terry Bradshaw. The two players became the team's offensive and defensive leaders during the 1970s.

In 1972, the Steelers won their first-ever division title. Their first-round playoff game against Oakland featured one of the most famous plays in NFL history, the "Immaculate Reception." With 22 seconds left, Pittsburgh trailed, 7–6. On fourth down, Bradshaw scrambled, then hurled a pass far downfield. An Oakland defensive back broke up the play, and the ball flew into the air. Steelers rookie running back Franco Harris, trailing the play, alertly snatched the ball just before it hit the turf. He ran downfield to score the winning touchdown.

Four Wins in Six Years

That win set the stage for the team's glory years. Anchored by the "Steel Curtain" defense, Pittsburgh won the Super Bowl in 1975, 1976, 1979, and 1980.

For more than a decade after their fourth win, however, the Steelers didn't do well. The Steelers' record improved when Bill Cowher replaced Noll in 1992, and the team made the playoffs six years in a row. The Steelers advanced to the Super Bowl in 1996 but lost to Dallas, 27–17. Their fifth Super Bowl win came a decade later and tied them with San Francisco and Dallas for the most Super Bowl triumphs.

Cowher retired after the 2006 season and was replaced by Mike Tomlin, making him just the team's third coach in nearly 40 years. The Rooney family still owns the team. The family's continuous ownership, coupled with the long **tenures** of the Steelers' coaches, have made the Steelers one of the league's most stable franchises.

(Go back to page 34.) ◀◀

The NFL's Best Safeties

In 1994, on the 75th anniversary of the founding of the NFL, a group of reporters and league officials voted for the best all-time players at each position. Three players were picked as the best safeties.

Ronnie Lott topped the list. During his 14-year NFL career, this USC graduate played for San Francisco, Los Angeles, and New York. He led the league in interceptions twice, had five seasons with at least 100 tackles, and was named All-Pro eight times. Lott's reputation, however, rests mainly on something that can't be measured; he is regarded as the hardest hitter ever to play his position.

Like Lott, Ken Houston played for 14 years. Houston first played with the Houston Oilers and then with the Washington Redskins. He was an All-Pro three times and played in the Pro Bowl 12 years in a row. In 1971, Houston returned four interceptions and a fumble for touchdowns.

Larry Wilson, a seventh-round draft choice, played his entire 13-year career for the St. Louis Cardinals. A six-time All-Pro and eight-time Pro Bowler, Wilson was especially noted for his toughness. He played part of one season with casts on both arms because of broken wrists.

Since 1994, other outstanding safeties have emerged. One of them is John Lynch. Lynch's career began in 1993, and he soon acquired a reputation as an especially hard hitter. Lynch was named to the All-Pro team four years in a row and is a nine-time Pro Bowler—five times with the Tampa Bay Buccaneers and four with the Denver Broncos.

Brian Dawkins of the Philadelphia Eagles is another great safety. A five-time All-Pro and six-time Pro Bowler, Dawkins is the only player in NFL history to record an interception, recover a fumble, sack the quarterback, and catch a touchdown pass in the same game.

A two-time All-American at the University of Miami, Ed Reed of the Baltimore Ravens was the AP NFL Defensive Player of the Year in 2004—the first time in 20 years that a safety had received this honor. He was named an All-Pro and voted to the Pro Bowl in four of his first five seasons.

Bob Sanders of the Indianapolis Colts was nicknamed "the Hitman" for his hard tackling and "the Eraser" because his play "erases" teammates' mistakes. He was the AP NFL Defensive Player of the Year in 2007, his fourth year in the league. Sanders is also a two-time All-Pro and Pro Bowler.

(Go back to page 39.)

Bob Sanders, strong safety for the Indianapolis Colts, stops Baltimore Ravens running back Mike Anderson in an AFC divisional playoff game, January 13, 2007. Though just 5'8" tall, Sanders is a fierce tackler.

Saipan and Okinawa

During World War II, some of the most brutal fighting between Japanese and American troops occurred on the islands of Saipan and Okinawa.

On June 15, 1944, U.S. Marines landed on Japanese-held Saipan. It took nearly four weeks before the Americans had secured the Central Pacific island. The cost was high—almost 3,000 U.S. servicemen were killed, and more than 10,000 were wounded. Japanese losses, however, were far heavier. Nearly all of the island's 30,000 Japanese defenders died, as did thousands of civilians. Many Japanese committed suicide rather than surrender.

The battle for Okinawa—less than 400 miles from the southernmost of Japan's main islands—began in late March 1945 and lasted nearly three months. It was the bloodiest battle in the Pacific.

During the battle, the Japanese fought desperately. Kamikazes—Japanese pilots who flew suicide missions, crashing their planes into U.S. naval vessels—sank or damaged at least 400 American ships and killed more than 5,000 sailors. This was twice the number of sailors who had died in the Japanese attack on Pearl Harbor, which had drawn the United States into World War II in December 1941. But the land fighting at Okinawa was even more brutal. U.S. casualties numbered more than 40,000, while the Japanese lost more than 100,000 men. Thousands of Okinawan civilians also perished before the 82-day battle was over in June 1945. (Go back to page 40.) ◄◄

The Eastern Orthodox Church

Troy Polamalu converted to Eastern Orthodoxy, his wife's faith. The roots of this faith lie in the early history of the Christian church.

A short time after the Christian religion was founded, tension arose among its followers. Much of this tension was due to the fact that the Christian church developed around two very different centers. One center was in Rome, in modern-day Italy. The other was in Constantinople, in modern-day Turkey. Each center had different ideas on how best to worship. Each center also had differences in culture and language. The language of the western center (Rome) was Latin, while in the eastern center (Constantinople) Greek was used. These differences led to the Great Schism in 1054. At that time, Christianity officially split into the Church of the West, now known as Roman Catholicism, and the Eastern Orthodox Church.

Today the Eastern Orthodox Church is the second-largest branch of Christianity, after Roman Catholicism. It is larger than any Protestant denomination. Most followers of this church, however, don't refer to their church as being Eastern Orthodox. Instead, they call it by the name of the country in which they live. For example, Russians belong to the Russian Orthodox Church, and Greeks to the Greek Orthodox Church.

All followers of this faith, however, have one belief in common. They believe they worship in the way Jesus Christ intended. (Go back to page 42.) ◄◄

1981   Troy Polamalu Aumua is born on April 19 in Garden Grove, California.

1989   Troy moves to Tenmile, Oregon, to live with his uncle's family.

1996   Troy rushes for more than 1,000 yards as a sophomore at Douglas High School; he achieves the same milestone the following year.

1998   Injuries limit Troy to just four games in his senior season at Douglas High School.

1999   Troy graduates from Douglas High School and enters the University of Southern California (USC) in the fall. He plays in eight games as a freshman.

2000   Troy becomes a starter at safety for USC and cuts his hair for the last time.

2001   Troy is named team captain for USC.

2002   Troy is captain again for USC, and he helps lead his team to the Orange Bowl. However, he misses almost the entire Orange Bowl game because of a hamstring injury.

2003   Troy is drafted in the first round by the Pittsburgh Steelers. He is the 16th pick overall.

2004   Troy moves into the starting lineup for Pittsburgh.

2005   Troy marries Theodora Holmes on January 27.

In the fall, Troy plays a vital role on the Steelers team, and the Steelers become AFC champions.

2006   Troy helps Pittsburgh win Super Bowl XL on February 5.

2007   Troy legally changes his name to Troy Polamalu.

Troy signs a four-year, $30 million contract extension.

Troy establishes the Harry Panos Fund to help soldiers injured in Iraq.

2008   Troy is picked for the Pro Bowl, but he chooses not to play because of a sprained knee.

1998 Named to the Super Prep All-Northwest team and the *Tacoma News Tribune* Western 100, which consists of the top 100 high school players in the western United States

2001 Named to many All-American teams

2002 One of three finalists for Jim Thorpe Award; named to many All-American teams

2003 Wins Joe Greene Great Performance Award as Pittsburgh's top rookie

2004 Second-team All-Pro selection; named to Pro Bowl

2005 First-team All-Pro selection; named to Pro Bowl

2006 Named to Pro Bowl

2007 Second-team All-Pro selection; named to Pro Bowl; named the Downtown [Pittsburgh] YMCA's Person of the Year

Career Statistics

YEAR	TEAM	G	TOT	SOLO	AST	PD	SACK	FF	REC	INT	YDS	TD
2003	PIT	16	38	32	6	4	2.0	1	0	0	0	0
2004	PIT	16	97	74	23	14	1.0	1	0	5	58	1
2005	PIT	16	92	74	18	8	3.0	1	78	2	42	0
2006	PIT	13	77	57	20	8	1.0	1	0	3	51	0
2007	PIT	11	58	45	13	9	0.0	3	13	0	0	0
Career		**72**	**362**	**282**	**80**	**43**	**7.0**	**7**	**0**	**10**	**151**	**1**

KEY

TOT = Total tackles

SOLO = Solo tackles

AST = Assisted tackles

PD = Pass deflections

FF = Forced fumbles

REC = Yards gained after fumble recoveries

INT = Interceptions

Books

Giglio, Joe. *Great Teams in Pro Football History* (*Great Teams* series). Chicago: Raintree, 2006.

Kelley, K. C. *AFC North*. (*Inside the NFL* series). Mankato, MN: Child's World, 2008.

Madden, John. *John Madden's Heroes of Football*. New York: Dutton Juvenile, 2006.

Rasmussen, Peter Anthony. *Trojans 2002: Return to Glory*. Champaign, IL: Sports Publishing LLC, 2003.

Stewart, Mark. *The Pittsburgh Steelers* (*Team Spirit* series). Chicago: Norwood House Press, 2006.

Zuehlke, Jeffrey. *Ben Roethlisberger* (*Amazing Athletes* series). Minneapolis: Lerner Books, 2007.

Web Sites

http://usctrojans.cstv.com/sports/m-footbl/mtt/polamalu_troy00.html

This Web site gives a summary of Troy Polamalu's career at the University of Southern California, with game-by-game statistics, comments, and quotes from Troy.

http://www.steelers.com/

The official Web site of the Pittsburgh Steelers has the team's roster, schedule, statistics, news, merchandise, and more.

http://www.youtube.com/watch?v=07zsdF0ysP0&NR=1

This video shows the "Immaculate Reception," the famous touchdown catch made by Steeler Franco Harris against Oakland in the 1972 NFL playoffs.

http://www.steelersfever.com/editorials/0757.html

This Pittsburgh Steelers fan site has news articles, team statistics, team history, NFL links, and more.

http://www.youtube.com/watch?v=tqWVXuKUd64

This video shows an interview in which Troy shares feelings about his contract, Pittsburgh, and more.

http://www.profootballhof.com/

The official Web site of the Pro Football Hall of Fame lists all the players who have been inducted and offers video tours, photo galleries, a history of pro football, visitor information, and merchandise.

The Web sites mentioned in this book were active at the time of publication. The publisher is not responsible for Web sites that have changed their addresses or discontinued operation since the date of publication. The publisher will review and update the Web site addresses each time the book is reprinted.

analyst—in sports, a person who studies in detail and evaluates the performance of players and/or teams.

Apostles—early followers of Jesus Christ who spread the Christian religion.

blitz—a defensive play in which one or more defensive backs rush the quarterback and attempt to tackle him for a loss of yards or force him to throw the ball before he is ready.

chicanery—trickery; deception.

contract—an agreement between two parties. In the NFL, these agreements are between players and teams and involve decisions on how many years the player will play for a specific team and how much the team will pay the player.

culmination—the final or most important point in an activity.

defensive back—a football player who is mainly responsible for covering receivers on pass plays. Defensive backs include safeties and cornerbacks.

draft—the process by which NFL teams select new team members from the nation's top college football players.

integrity—adherence to a set of values or a moral code of conduct.

mentor—a teacher or respected adviser.

Pac-10 Conference—an association of sports teams from 10 universities in the western United States. The association organizes games among its members and sponsors 11 men's and women's sports.

recruit—to attempt to convince a top high school football player to attend a specific college and play for that college's team.

safety—a defensive back who either helps cover a receiver directly or plays a particular area of the field in an attempt to prevent passes from being completed.

scout—a person who works for a specific team and whose job it is to look for talented athletes to play on that team.

secondary—the group of defensive football players who line up behind the defensive linemen. The secondary includes defensive backs.

special teams—the group of players who enter the game for kickoffs, punts, field goals, and points after a touchdown. These players are often second- and third-string players.

tenure—length of service with a particular organization.

Chapter 1: Super Bowl Champion

page 5   "[Troy] does things . . ." Jim Corbett, "Polamalu's Sudden Impact Revolutionizing Safety Position," *USA Today* (February 15, 2006). http://www.usatoday.com/sports/football/nfl/steelers/2006-02-15-polamalu-feature_x.htm

page 7   "There isn't a safety . . ." Tom Silverstein, "Polamalu Found His Escape in Sports," *Milwaukee Journal Sentinel* (February 2, 2006). http://www.accessmylibrary.com/coms2/summary_0286-31702667_ITM

page 7   "[Troy has] more disguises . . ." Nunyo Demasio, "The Devil Gets His Due: Steelers' Polamalu's Unique Style Changes the Game," *SI.com* (January 30, 2006). http://sportsillustrated.cnn.com/2006/writers/nunyo_demasio/01/30/polamalu/index.html

page 7   "Sometimes he'll run from deep . . ." Greg Garber, "Smallish Defenders Consistently Making Big Plays," *ESPN.com* (February 2, 2006). http://sports.espn.go.com/nfl/playoffs05/news/story?id=2315311

page 8   "The Steelers used Polamalu . . ." Associated Press, "Pittsburgh's Polamalu a One-of-a-kind Defender, *NBCSports.msnbc.com* (January 19, 2006). http://nbcsports.msnbc.com/id/10930232/

page 9   "The Seahawks' only touchdown . . ." Dan Pompei, "Big Shoes Left Unfilled," *Sportingnews.com* (February 7, 2006). http://www.sportingnews.com/yourturn/viewtopic.php?t=60076

page 9   "the most valuable defensive . . ." Corbett, "Polamalu's Sudden Impact."

Chapter 2: Ten Years in Tenmile

page 11   "I saw cows . . ." David Kamp, "Troy Story," *GQ* (September 2006), 407.

page 12   "[Troy's] so intelligent . . ." Silverstein, "Polamalu Found His Escape."

page 13   "[Salu] is a disciplinarian . . ." Gerry Dulac, "Steelers, First-round Pick Polamalu Dance to Same Beat," *Pittsburgh Post-Gazette* (April 27, 2003). http://www.post-gazette.com/steelers/20030427one0427p4.asp

page 13   "I knew that I had . . ." Lee Jenkins, "Polamalu Dances with Fire, Just Not in the End Zone," *New York Times* (January 20, 2005). http://www.nytimes.com/2005/01/20/sports/football/20steelers.html

page 13   "Polamalu became a straight-A . . ." Ibid.

page 14   "[Troy] was probably better . . ." Ibid.

page 14   "Troy killed us . . ." Steve Mims, "The Roots of a Hometown HERO," *The Register-Guard* (Eugene, Oregon) (February 1, 2006). http://www.thefreelibrary.com/The+roots+of+a+hometown+HERO.(Sports)(Fans+of+Douglas+High+School...-a0141652688

page 15   "You'd put him back defensively. . ." Ibid.

page 15   "To hear him talk . . ." Craig Reed, "Troy Polamalu's Roots: Remembering Back When," *The News-Review* (Roseburg, Oregon) (February 2, 2006). http://www.nrtoday.com/article/200602 02/SPORTS/60202028&SearchID=7332 2040081241&parentprofile=search

Chapter 3: Troy the USC Trojan

page 17   "So he goes out there . . ." Mike Wilkening, "Big Hitter: USC's Troy Polamalu Helped

Spark Resurgent Season for Trojans," *Pro Football Weekly* (December 26, 2002). http://www.profootballweekly.com/PFW/NFLDraft/Draft+Extras/2002/profile122602.htm

page 19 "The thing that's really hard . . ." Ibid.

page 20 "I had to establish . . ." "Troy Polamalu Profile," The University of Southern California Trojans—Official Athletic Site. http://usctrojans.cstv.com/sports/m-footbl/mtt/polamalu_troy00.html

page 22 "The guys that light . . ." Peter Anthony Rasmussen, *Trojans 2002: Return to Glory* (Champaign, IL: Sports Publishing LLC, 2003), 10.

page 25 "He's an incredible . . ." Manny Navarro, "USC's Polamalu Leaving a Mark," *Miami Herald* (December 28, 2002).

Chapter 4: Rising to the Top

page 29 "[Troy] plays for his faith . . ." Dulac, "Steelers, First-round Pick."

page 29 "It's sort of how you . . ." Jenkins, "Polamalu Dances with Fire."

page 29 "My rookie year . . ." Gerry Dulac, "Polamalu More Than Meets Eye: Steelers Safety a Bundle of Energy on Field; Quiet and Thoughtful off of It," *Southcoasttoday.com* (February 3, 2006). http://archive.southcoasttoday.com/daily/02-06/02-03-06/c01sp998.htm

page 30 "He gives you unlimited flexibility . . ." Judy Battista, "Pittsburgh Safety Could Lurk Anywhere Against Seattle," *New York Times* (January 30, 2006). http://www.nytimes.com/2006/01/30/sports/football/30steelers.html

page 30 "It goes with the way . . ." Nunyo Demasio, "The Mane Man," *SI.com* (November 14, 2005). http://vault.sportsillustrated.cnn.com/vault/article/magazine/MAG1105646/index.htm

page 31 "I couldn't have been happier . . ." Tom Eggers, "Pittsburgh's Troy Polamalu: Soft as Steel," *The News-Review* (Roseburg, Oregon) (February 4, 2006). http://www.nrtoday.com/article/20060204/NEWS/60204002

page 32 "It's nice to be able . . ." Ibid.

page 34 "Polamalu tackled Denver . . ." Battista, "Pittsburgh Safety Could Lurk."

page 35 "I was out of position . . ." Dulac, "Polamalu More Than Meets Eye."

page 35 "No question [the Steelers] . . ." Larry Weisman, "It's Steel Curtains for Seahawks in Super Bowl XL," *USA Today* (February 5, 2006). http://www.usatoday.com/sports/football/super/2006-02-05-seahawks-steelers_x.htm

Chapter 5: A Bright Future

page 36 "I mean, the dude had . . ." Robert Dvorchak, "Steelers Victory Had Everything, Including a Bizarre Hair Tackle," *Pittsburgh Post-Gazette* (October 16, 2006). http://www.post-gazette.com/pg/06289/730386-66.stm

page 37 "He can tackle me. . ." Ibid.

page 39 "[Troy] used his incredible . . ." Ron Cook, "Steelers Have to Sign Polamalu to Be Fair to Tomlin," *Pittsburgh Post-Gazette* (May 20, 2007). http://www.post-gazette.com/pg/07140/787610-87.stm

page 39 "I didn't want to be . . ." "Steelers Lock up Polamalu Through 2011 Season," *ESPN.com* (July 23, 2007). http://sports.espn.go.com/nfl/news/story?id=2946532

page 40 "When Troy went to . . ." "Two More Steelers Create Funds at The Pittsburgh Foundation," The Pittsburgh Foundation (July 16, 2007). http://www.pittsburghfoundation.org/page8852.cfm

page 42 "You can truly save . . ." Ed Bouchette, "Polamalu's Unique Spirit Uplifting for Steelers, Fans," *Pittsburgh Post-Gazette* (August 1, 2006). http://www.post-gazette.com/pg/06213/710094-66.stm

page 42 "He participates in a lot . . ." Jim O'Brien, "Troy Polamalu Goes on Holy Pilgrimage," *The Almanac.net* (April 18, 2007). http://orp.live.mediaspanonline.com/ALM/Story/O__Brien_Polamalu_4_18

page 42 "What's really neat about . . ." Jason Cole, "Tuesday Conversation: Troy Polamalu," *Yahoo! Sports* (September 25, 2007). http://sports.yahoo.com/nfl/news?slug=jc-tuesdayconversation092507

page 42 "I don't view football . . ." Corbett, "Polamalu's Sudden Impact."

page 43 "I know I have been identified . . ." Ibid.

page 45 "With my life, there's no way. . ." Kamp, "Troy Story," 408.

page 45 "I do share different passions. . ." Chris Harlan, "Passion of the Safety," *Beaver County Times* (January 21, 2005) http://blackandgoldworld.blogspot.com/2005_01_16_archive.html

Cross-Currents

page 48 "the sport we were born . . ." Ted Miller, "American Football, Samoan Style," *ESPN.com*, May 31, 2007. http://espn.go.com/gen/s/2002/0527/1387562.html

page 49 "I honestly think . . ." Greg Garber, "The Dominican Republic of the NFL," *ESPN.com* (May 28, 2002). http://espn.go.com/gen/s/2002/0527/1387626.html

page 49 "by-product of the original . . ." Ibid.

Numbers in ***bold italics*** refer to captions.

Jim Whiting has written more than 100 children's nonfiction books and edited well over 150 more during an especially diverse writing career. He published *Northwest Runner* magazine for more than 17 years. His other credits include advising a national award-winning high school newspaper, sports editor for the *Bainbridge Island Review*, event and venue write-ups and photography for American Online, articles in dozens of magazines, light verse in the *Saturday Evening Post*, the first piece of original fiction to appear in *Runner's World*, and the official photographer for the Antarctica Marathon.

PICTURE CREDITS

page

5: beejayreyes/AASI Photos

6: David P. Gilkey/Detroit Free Press/KRT

8: Matthew K./AASI Photos

11: USC/SPCS

12: ragart/T&T/IOA Photos

17: USC/SPCS

18: Cathy P./AASI Photos

21: USC/SPCS

23: USC/SPCS

24: USC/SPCS

27: USC/SPCS

28: Tom Murphy VII/T&T/IOA Photos

31: Ken Love/Akron Beacon Journal/KRT

33: Sports Illustrated/NMI

34: Julian H. Gonzalez/Detroit Free Press/KRT

37: John Sleezer/Kansas City Star/MCT

38: Bob DeMay/Akron Beacon Journal/MCT

41: Kevin Reece/Icon SMI

43: Nike/NMI

44: Streeter Lecka/Getty Images

46: George Bridges/MCT

48: WSU/SPCS

53: George Bridges/MCT

Front cover: Al Tielemans/Sports Illustrated/Getty Images

Front cover inset: Pittsburgh Steelers/PRMS